FOLLOWING HIS ORDERS

IMPERIAL STORMTROOPERS ALWAYS
FOLLOW THE ORDERS OF LORD VADER.
WHICH STORMTROOPER IS DIFFERENT?

Dalmatian Press

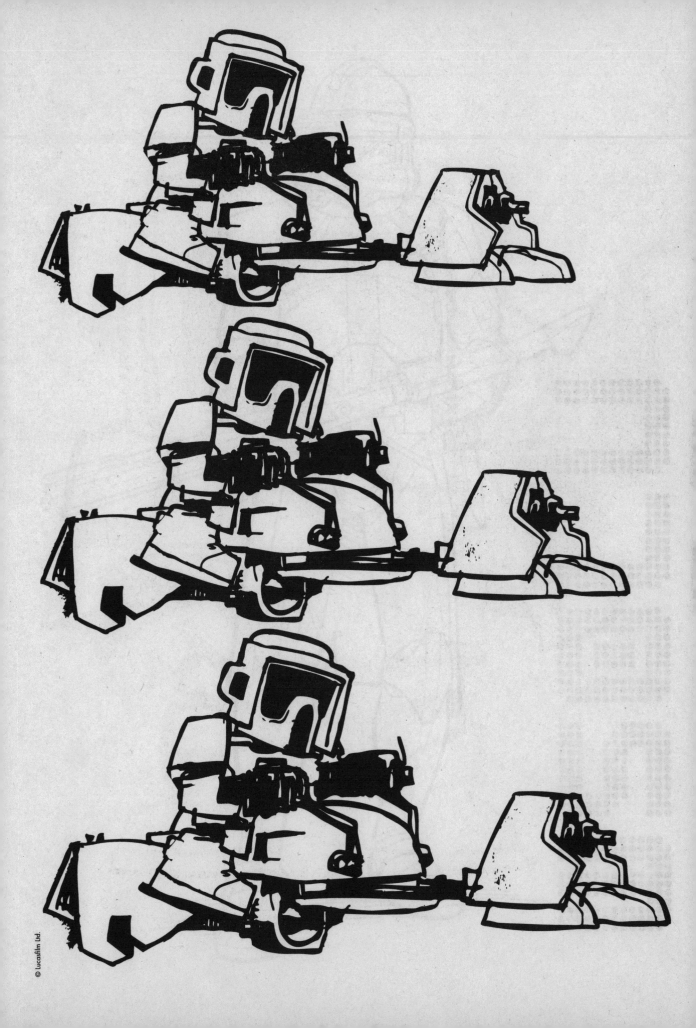

"THERE'S ONE!
SET FOR STUN."

"INFORM LORD
VADER, WE HAVE
A PRISONER."

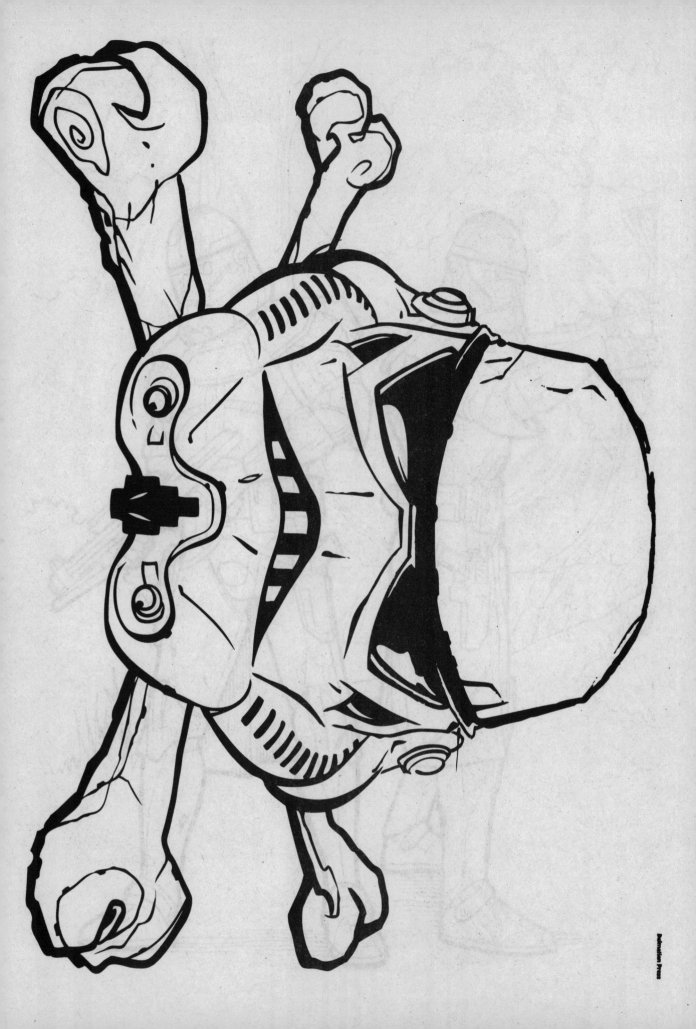

AT-AT

ALL TERRAIN ARMORED TRANSPORT

Dalmatian Press

WOOKIEES

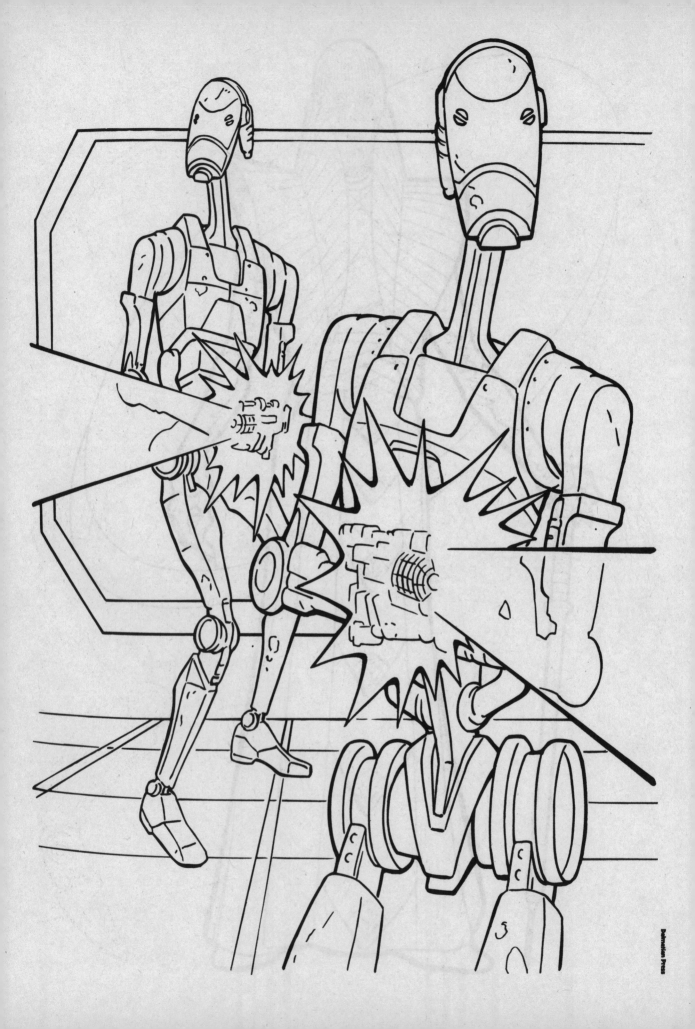

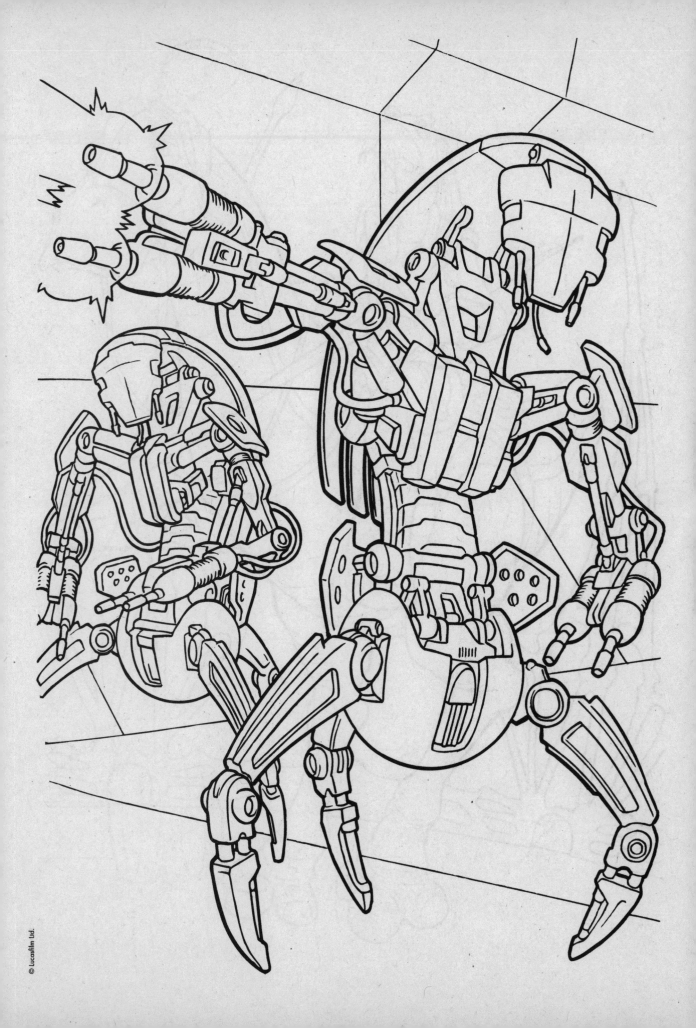

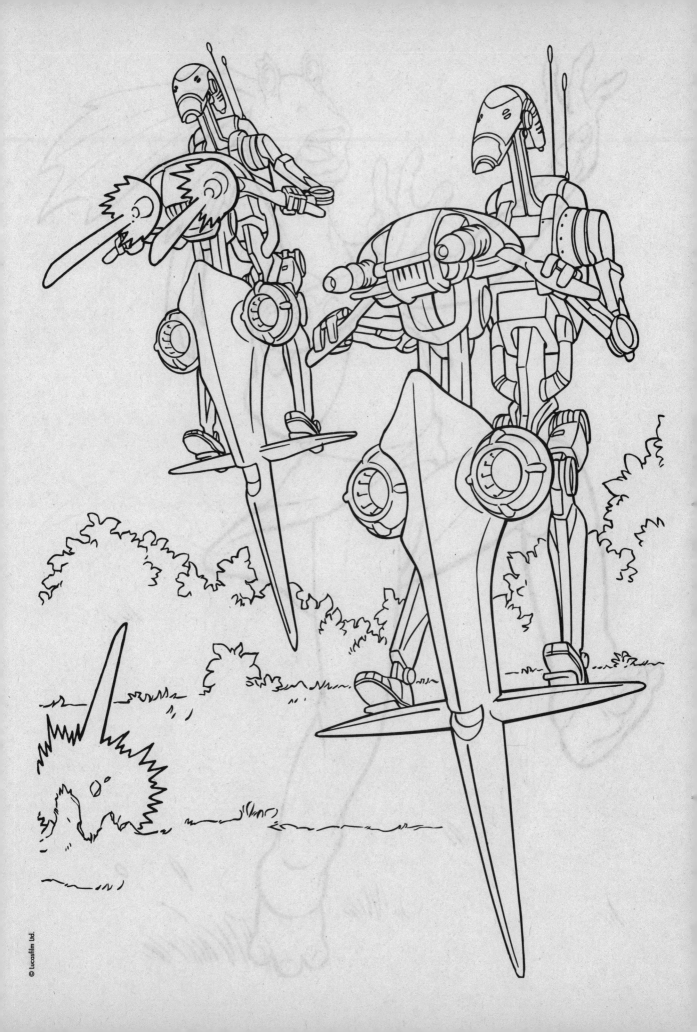

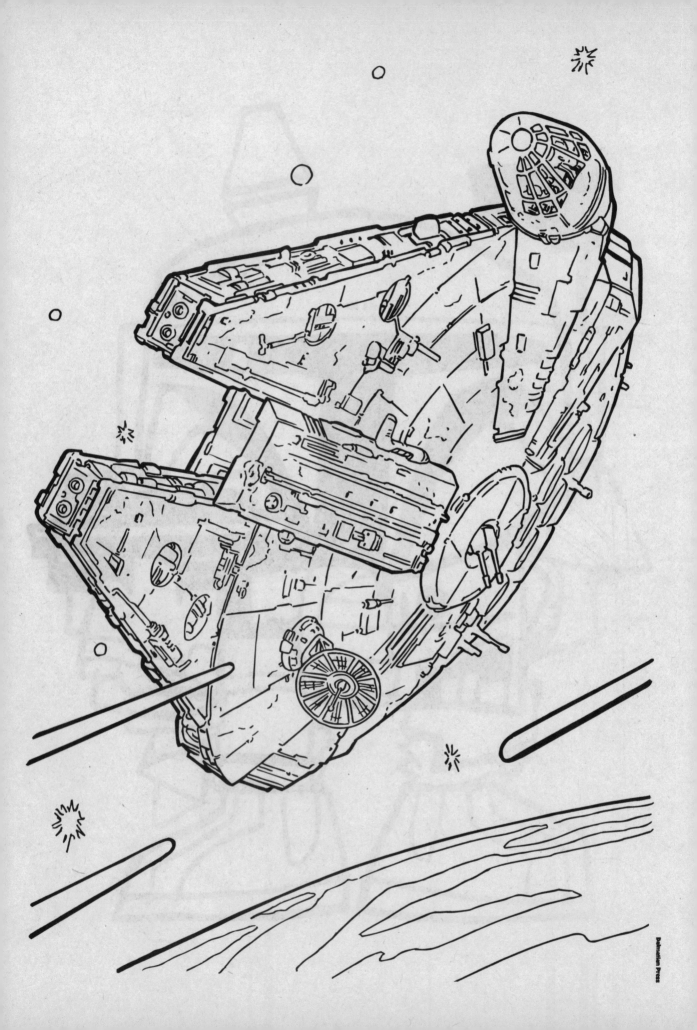

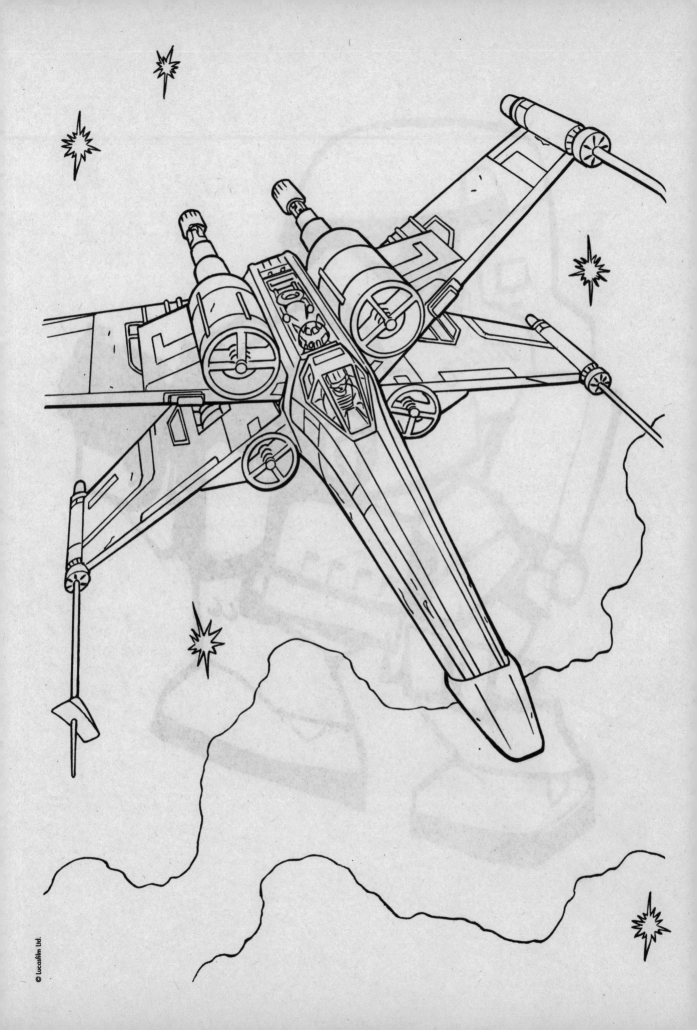

TIE Fighter

TWIN ION ENGINE

OBI-WAN

ORDER 66

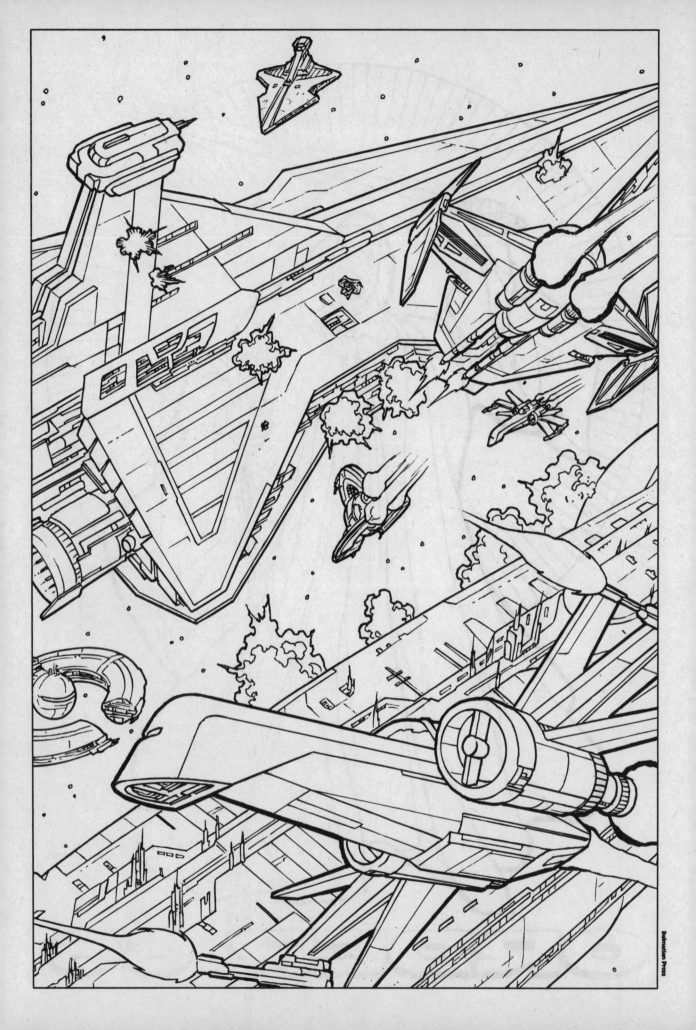

DARTH SIDIOUS

QUI-GON JINN

MACE WINDU

PRINCESS
LEIA
ORGANA

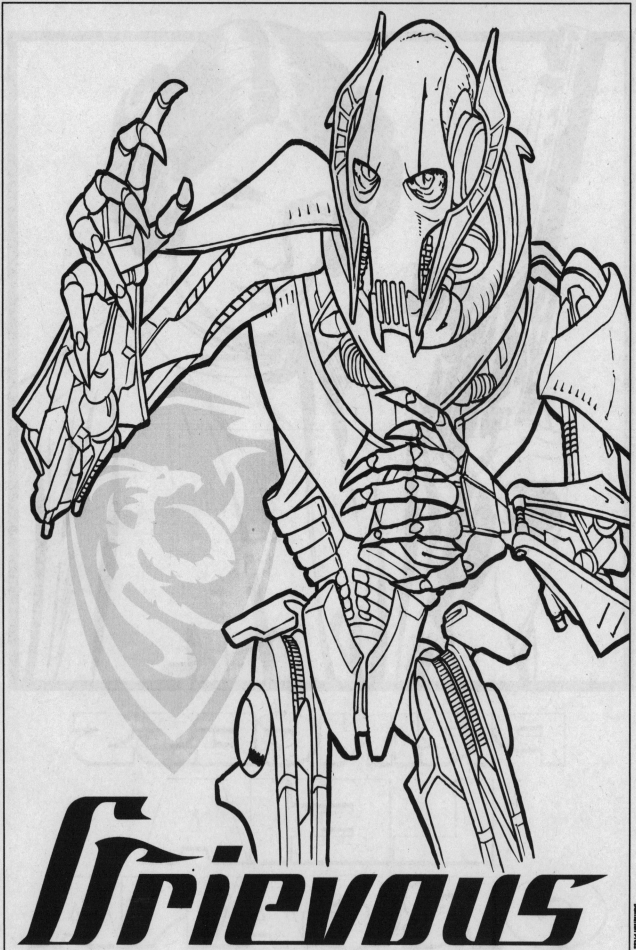

Grievous

Definition Press

JEDI

COMPLETE YOUR TRAINING.

**A LIGHTSABER IS AN IMPORTANT PART OF A JEDI'S WEAPONRY.
COMPLETE AND COLOR JEDI MASTER YODA'S LIGHTSABER.**